D1614345

Searchlight
BOOKS™

Predators

Orcas

on the Hunt

Alicia Z. Klepeis

Lerner Publications • Minneapolis

Content Consultant: Jennifer B. Tennessen, PhD, Research Associate, Department of
Biology, Western Washington University

Lerner Publications Company
A division of Lerner Publishing Group, Inc.
241 First Avenue North
Minneapolis, MN 55401 USA

For reading levels and more information, look up this title at
www.lernerbooks.com.

Library of Congress Cataloging-in-Publication Data

The Cataloging-in-Publication Data for *Orcas on the Hunt* is on file at the Library of
Congress.
ISBN 978-1-5124-3398-2 (lib. bdg.)
ISBN 978-1-5124-5609-7 (pbk.)
ISBN 978-1-5124-5080-4 (EB pdf)

Manufactured in the United States of America
1 — CG — 7/15/17

Contents

Chapter 1

ON THE HUNT

It is an overcast evening off the coast of Antarctica. A freezing cold breeze blows. A pod, or group, of orcas swims just below the waves. Their large dorsal fins loom above the water's surface. The orcas swim over to some ice floes, or sheets of floating ice. They are hunting for seals, which rest on ice floes between dives for food.

A pod of orcas swims through the Antarctic sea ice looking for food. What are they hunting?

The orcas lift their heads out of the water. One of the pod members spots a crabeater seal lying on an ice floe. But the seal is not safe even out of the water.

One orca moves in. This adult female orca is huge. She is four times as long as the crabeater seal. The other members of her pod have noticed the seal now and come closer. They will work together to catch the seal.

Orcas bring their heads above water to find seals on ice. This is called spy hopping.

The Catch

The female orca pushes her body against the ice floe, turning it around. Members of the pod also move some other nearby pieces of ice away. They move the floe into the perfect position to wash the seal off of it.

The adult orcas line up perfectly. They charge the ice floe, creating a big wave. This wave washes the seal off the floe, where hungry orcas are waiting to catch it by its tail.

Orcas swim up to and dive under the ice floe, using their tails to push the wave over the ice.

THE WAVE PUSHES THE SEAL TOWARD A WAITING ORCA.

▼

The seal tries to escape, but the orca's 4-inch-long (10 centimeter) teeth keep a tight grip on it. Underwater, the orcas tear and eat chunks of seal. After finishing the seal, the orcas swim off in search of their next meal.

Chapter 2

WHERE ORCAS LIVE

Orcas are the most widely distributed marine mammals in the world. They live in every ocean, from the polar regions to the equator. Orcas are most abundant in colder waters, such as those of Antarctica, the North Atlantic, and parts of the Pacific Ocean. Orcas often live in thinner numbers in tropical, subtropical, and offshore waters.

This orca swims in Puget Sound along the Washington State coast. Where do orcas live?

There are about 50,000 orcas on Earth. In the Southern Hemisphere, orcas are common off the coasts of South Africa, New Zealand, Argentina, and the Galápagos Islands. In the Northern Hemisphere, they are found in the Pacific Ocean off the coasts of North America and Russia. In the North Atlantic, they are found off the coasts of Newfoundland and Labrador, the British Isles, Iceland, and Norway.

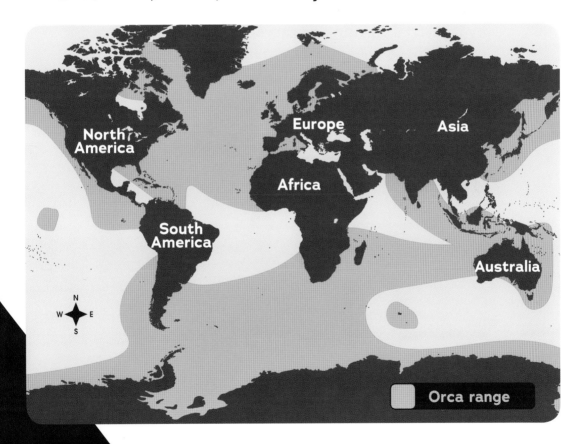

North America

Europe

Asia

Africa

South America

Australia

N
W   E
S

Orca range

Threats to Orcas

Orcas are the ocean's top predators. Yet they still face challenges. When humans overfish in an area, it can decrease the supply of fish some orcas eat. Collisions with ships and becoming tangled in fishing gear can injure orcas. Loud noises created by industrial, military, or recreational activities also disturb these animals. These noises make it harder for orcas to hear prey and communicate with each other across distances. Toxins dumped into the oceans can also harm orcas.

A boat or ship's engine creates noise pollution.

Orcas in some areas leap out of the water more frequently than other orcas. This act is called breaching.

Differences around the Globe

All orcas belong to the same species, *Orcinus orca*. But scientists who study cetaceans have found that there are differences between some groups of orcas. These differences depend on where the orcas live. Orcas living near Norway often communicate using different sounds than those living near Antarctica. The hunting strategies they use differ depending on where they live and what they eat. As scientists learn more about these differences, they may divide orcas into several species in the future.

Orcas and Humans

Regardless of where they live, orcas are the apex predators in the ocean. They are at the top of the ocean food chain. Orcas can even win conflicts with great white sharks. Humans have usually respected orcas and left them alone throughout history. The Tlingit from southern Alaska and the Coast Salish from coastal Washington, Oregon, and British Columbia, Canada, have traditional stories that explain the world around them. Both nations have featured orcas in their art and in their stories.

An orca sits on top of a Tlingit totem pole.

Chapter 3

ORCA FEATURES

Over time, orcas have adapted to life in cold waters. Their blubber acts as a winter coat to protect them against the frigid water temperatures. Blubber keeps them warm while they hunt for prey in cold waters.

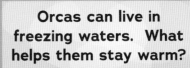

Orcas can live in freezing waters. What helps them stay warm?

The saddle patch can vary in its shade of gray.

Saddle Patch

Appearance

It is easy to tell an orca from other marine animals. There are many ideas about how orcas got their name. The term *orca* is Latin for "the shape of a barrel or cask," so this term may have been adopted to describe its body shape. An orca has a large, black body with a white underside, as well as a white patch behind and above the eye. A gray area called a saddle patch sits behind the dorsal fin. Every orca's saddle patch is different.

An orca's unusual color pattern helps it hunt. Its black and white colors camouflage it. Animals below an orca see its white belly, which blends in with the sunlight streaming into the water above. Animals above see the orca's black back, which blends in with the dark water below.

Male and female orcas can be identified by their fins. Males have a taller, straighter dorsal fin that can be more than 6 feet (1.8 meters) in height. The female's dorsal fin is smaller and has more of a curved, sickle-like shape.

Male orcas have taller dorsal fins than any other marine mammal.

Female

Male

Size, Speed, and Senses

Orcas are huge animals. They can measure 23 to 32 feet (7 to 9.8 m) long. That is as long as a two- to three-story house is tall. Males are significantly larger than females. They can weigh up to 22,000 pounds (10,000 kilograms), which is about as heavy as a school bus. Females can weigh up to 16,500 pounds (7,500 kg).

Despite their size, orcas are fast swimmers. They can swim up to 30 miles (48 kilometers) per hour and tend to swim fastest when on the hunt. When they are not hunting, orcas usually swim 3 to 4 miles (4.8 to 6.4 km) per hour.

Orcas reach their top speeds when on the hunt.

Since visibility underwater is often poor, orcas rely more on their other senses.

Orcas have keen senses. They have great vision both in and out of the water. However, sight is of limited use to them. Orcas spend lots of time in deep, dark ocean water. A good sense of hearing is more important in these places. These marine animals can hear a wide range of sounds. They have small holes behind their eyes that act as ears. Orcas may also be able to use their lower jaws to sense sounds.

Orca Intelligence

Orcas are intelligent. They use different hunting strategies for different kinds of prey. They pass these strategies down to the next generation of orcas. Scientists tested orcas using the EQ scale. The EQ scale compares an animal's brain size with that of a similarly sized animal to estimate the animal's intelligence. Humans score a 7, and orcas score a 2.5 on the scale. Bottlenose dolphins score a 5.3, and dogs score a 1.2. Orcas are also one of the few animals that are likely able to recognize themselves in a mirror.

While orcas score high on the EQ scale, bottlenose dolphins score among the highest of any animal.

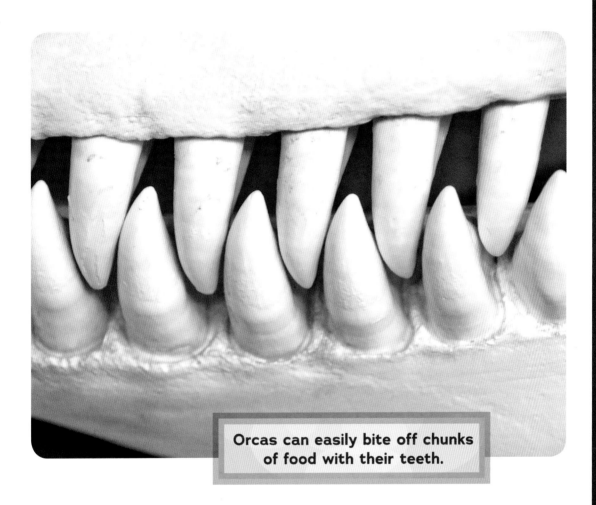

**Orcas can easily bite off chunks
of food with their teeth.**

One of the features that makes orcas such efficient predators is their set of teeth. Orcas have forty-eight to fifty-two cone-shaped teeth. Their teeth are interlocking and fit tightly together, allowing orcas to grip prey. But their teeth are not good at chewing food. Instead, orcas bite off chunks of food and swallow them whole!

Chapter 4

WOLVES OF THE SEA

Orcas have been called the wolves of the sea. Like wolves, orcas are highly social animals that live and hunt in groups, or pods. Scientists have identified three main types of orcas in the orca populations that live off the western coast of North America in the North Pacific. These three pod types are residents, transients, and offshores. In general, the different types of pods do not interact with each other.

Females lead orca pods. What types of pods are there in the North Pacific?

Resident Pods

Resident pods may have as many as fifty orcas. Mothers and their offspring form these pods. It is rare for them to leave. Resident orcas travel shorter distances than other orcas, feeding in areas with dense fish populations. Residents are also less aggressive during foraging than the whales in transient pods. These orcas share their food and spend around 50 to 67 percent of the daylight hours foraging for fish.

Resident orcas eat fish, such as salmon.

Transient orcas may swim up to shore to catch a sea lion.

Transient Orcas

Transient groups often have just a few members. They are usually made up of a mother and her sons and daughters. The daughters leave when they are old enough to reproduce and form their own pods.

Transient orcas roam far as they search for food. Some move between Southern California and the Arctic Circle. Transients feed on marine mammals such as porpoises, seals, and sea lions. They even attack whales larger than themselves. Members work together to hunt their prey. They spend up to 90 percent of their daylight hours looking for food.

Offshore and Others

Offshore orcas live from the Bering Sea to Southern California. These orcas are rarely encountered, and little is known about them, as they spend most of their time in the open ocean along the outer continental shelf. Offshore orcas prey on both fish and sharks. They typically live in large groups of more than thirty individuals.

Orcas around the world have similarities to these three types of orcas. They specialize in feeding on either fish or marine mammals and behave similarly to those living off the coast of North America.

Some orcas hunt sea birds, such as penguins.

Hunting

Orcas hunt in groups and use a wide variety of hunting techniques depending on their prey. They often use a carouseling technique when feeding on small fish such as herring. In this technique, a pod of orcas swims underneath and around a school of fish. They herd the fish into a bait ball, which looks like a rotating carousel. Then the orcas slap this ball with their tails. This kills or stuns the fish, making it easy for orcas to gulp them down.

Bait balls are tight schools of fish. Many large marine animals feed on them.

Orca Life

Orcas commonly live fifty to eighty years in the wild. Females reach maturity around fifteen years old, when they are about 15 to 18 feet (4.6 to 5.5 m) long. A female orca has an average of three to five calves throughout her life. Calves can be 8 feet (2.4 m) long and weigh almost 400 pounds (180 kg) at birth. Mother orcas and younger females in the pod work hard to protect and care for calves.

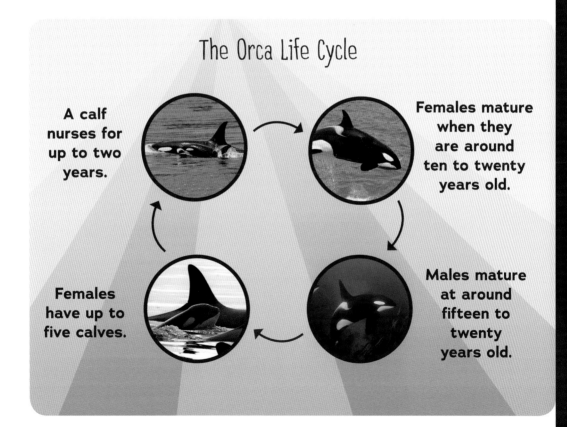

The Orca Life Cycle

A calf nurses for up to two years.

Females mature when they are around ten to twenty years old.

Males mature at around fifteen to twenty years old.

Females have up to five calves.

Echolocation

Echolocation is a way to locate objects using sound. This process is especially important in hunting. Orcas make clicking sounds that pass through a part of their head called the melon, which focuses these sounds into a narrow beam. These clicks travel underwater and then bounce back to the sender after hitting an object. This tells the orca the size and shape of the object, as well as where it is located. This technique also helps orcas figure out where they are in dark ocean water.

Melon

The orca's melon creates a bump on the top of its head.

Some orcas hunt baby gray whales.

Orcas communicate with each other using a wide variety of sounds. Each pod makes distinctive noises that its members will recognize. These sounds are called a dialect. Orcas make whistling sounds, clicks, and pulsed calls. The pulsed calls can sound like screams, squawks, and squeaks.

From the Arctic Circle to Antarctica, orcas are awesome hunters. They are fast, coordinated, and intelligent. Working in groups, these animals can hunt prey far larger than themselves. Orcas are powerful predators!

ORCA Fact File

Scientific Name: *Orcinus orca*

Where It Is Found: oceans around the world

Habitat: most marine areas, but more common in cold, coastal waters

Diet: varies depending on where the animals live, but includes fish, octopuses, squid, sea turtles, seals, sea lions, sea birds, whales, dolphins, and porpoises

Length: 23 to 32 feet (7–9.8 m) long

Weight: Males weigh up to 22,000 pounds (10,000 kg). Females weigh up to 16,500 pounds (7,500 kg).

Life Span: 50 to 80 years in the wild

Food Chain

Glossary

apex predator: an animal that has no natural predators and is at the top of a food chain

blubber: a layer of fat beneath the skin on a whale or other marine mammal

cetacean: a marine mammal in the order Cetacea, such as a whale, dolphin, or porpoise

continental shelf: the shallow plain of ocean floor off a continent's coast, which often ends with a sharp dip into deep ocean

dorsal fin: a long, flat fin located on an orca's back

marine: found in, related to, or produced by the ocean

pod: a group of animals, especially orcas

predator: an animal that survives by killing and eating other animals

prey: animals that other animals hunt and eat

recreational: done for entertainment

social: living in groups or communities

Learn More about Orcas

Books

Batten, Mary. *Baby Orca*. New York: Grosset & Dunlap, 2016. This book follows the life of a baby orca as it matures.

Fleisher, Paul. *Ocean Food Webs in Action*. Minneapolis: Lerner Publications Company, 2014. Discover how plants and animals in ocean ecosystems rely on each other to thrive.

Woodward, John. *Ocean: A Visual Encyclopedia*. New York: DK Publishing, 2015. Explore engaging photos illustrating facts readers need to know about oceans.

Websites

National Geographic: Orca
http://animals.nationalgeographic.com/animals/mammals/killer-whale/
See photos of orcas and find out fun facts and information about their hunting and communication techniques.

National Wildlife Federation: Ooh . . . Orcas!
https://www.nwf.org/Kids/Ranger-Rick/Animals/Mammals/Orcas.aspx
Learn about how orcas live. Engaging photos and illustrations expand on what the text discusses.

Public Broadcasting Service: The Killer Whale's Killer Weapon—Its Brain
http://www.pbs.org/wnet/nature/killer-whales-killer-weapon-brain/11352/
Find out many different hunting techniques used by orcas and watch several video clips of orcas hunting.

Index

Photo Acknowledgments

The images in this book are used with the permission of: © Ron Niebrugge/Alamy Stock Photo, p. 4; © vladsilver/iStock.com, pp. 5, 7; © Dorling Kindersley/Getty Images, p. 6; © RobynPhoto/iStock.com, p. 8; © Red Line Editorial, p. 9; © shaunl/iStock.com, p. 10; © Schaef1/iStock.com, p.11;©NigelHicks/DKImages,p.12;©pilipenkoD/iStock.com,p.13;©ChristianMusat/Shutterstock.com,pp. 14, 25 (top right); © Eric Middelkoop/iStock.com, p. 15; © blickwinke/Hummell/AlamyStockPhoto,p.16;©wildestanimal/Shutterstock.com,p.17;©ToryKallman/Shutterstock.com,p.18;©wwing/iStock.com,p.19;©cullenphotos/iStock.com,p.20;©Rasmus-Raahauge/iStock.com,pp.21, 25 (bottom right); © Francois Gohier/VWPics/Alamy Stock Photo, p.22;©S_Lew/iStock.com,p.23;©LeonardoGonzalez/Shutterstock.com,p.24;©MarkMalleson/iStock.com, p. 25 (top left); © Monika Wieland Shields/Shutterstock.com, p. 25 (bottom left); © Tom Middleton/Shutterstock.com,p.26;©FrancoisGohier/ScienceSource,p.27;©jamirae/iStock.com,p.29(top);©Vladimir Melnik/iStock.com,p.29(middletop);©pomarinus/iStock.com,p.29(middlebottom);©Videologia/iStock.com, p. 29 (bottom).

Front Cover: © Tory Kallman/Shutterstock.com.

Main body text set in Adrianna Regular 14/20.
Typeface provided by Chank.